Never Sell Yourself Short

Stephanie Riggs

PHOTOGRAPHS BY Bill Youmans

Albert Whitman & Company

Morton Grove, Illinois

Library of Congress Cataloging-in-Publication Data

Riggs, Stephanie.
Never sell yourself short / by Stephanie Riggs ;
photographs by Bill Youmans.
p. cm.
ISBN 0-8075-5563-0 (hardcover)
1. Achondroplasia — Juvenile literature.
2. Dwarfism — Juvenile literature. [1. Achondroplasia.
2. Dwarfs. 3. Physically handicapped.]
I. Youmans, Bill, ill. II. Title.
RJ482.A25 R53 2001 618.92'71 — dc21
2001000889

The design is by Pamela Kende.

For more information
about Albert Whitman & Company,
visit our web site at www.awhitmanco.com.

The pictures on pp. 8–11 are provided courtesy of
Josh's family; the pictures on pp. 24–25 are provided
courtesy of LPA, Inc.

To Billy Barty, the founder and former president of LPA, Inc. (Little
    People of America). He recently passed away, but his message,
    Never sell yourself short, lives on in all of us.

Thank you to Josh Maudlin for sharing his life, inspiring outlook, and
    time. I'm also grateful to Cara Egan and Leroy Bankowski of LPA
    and all the people who took part in this book. And a special
    thanks to Abby Levine, Senior Editor at Albert Whitman &
    Company, who put her heart into this project—S.R.

To my wife, Joan, and my daughter, Kylie: Thanks for always letting me
    "take one more."—B.Y.

In memory of my aunt, Elaine Rechter, and in honor of my parents,
    Roberta Steinhardt and Michael Maudlin.—J.M.

Hi, my name is Josh. I'm fourteen and

in the eighth grade. One thing I really appreciate

is a good night's sleep.

But like many "little people," I have trouble

breathing while I sleep.

So my doctor gave me this scary-looking mask to wear to bed.

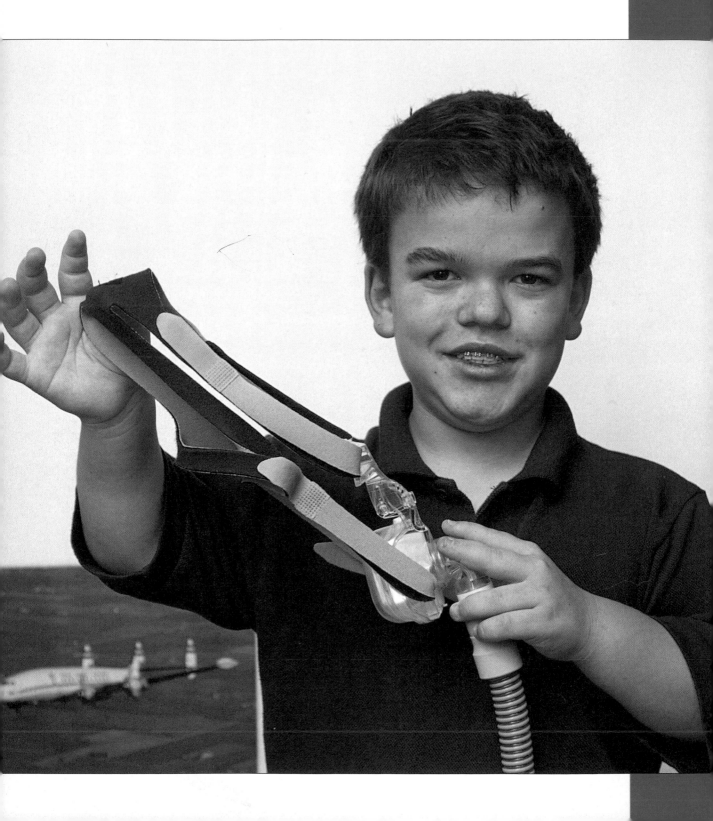

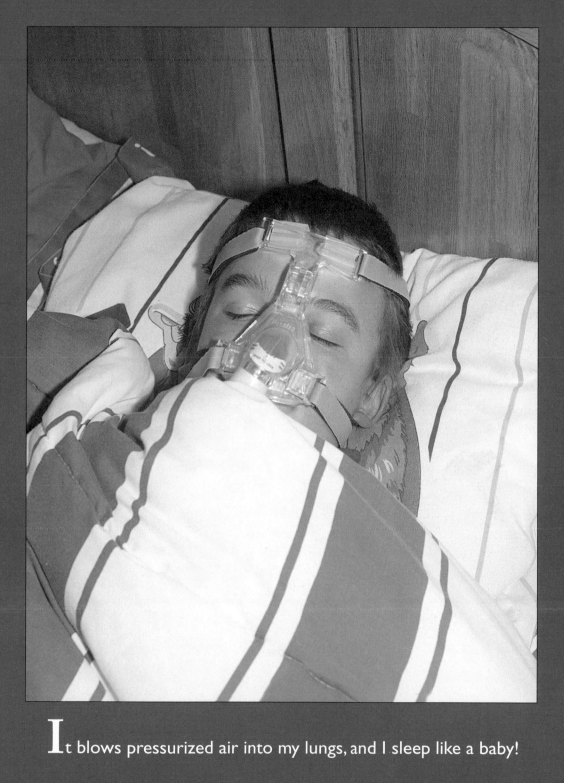

I t blows pressurized air into my lungs, and I sleep like a baby!

When I was a baby, doctors didn't know much about dwarfs. Today they know that there are more than one hundred types of dwarfism. Each type has its own physical challenges. I was born with achondroplasia (ay-kon-druh-PLAY-zhuh), the most common cause of short stature.

My mom and dad didn't care. They just thought I was really cute!

As I grew, I noticed my arms and legs didn't grow like those of other kids. That's because my form of dwarfism causes a person to have very short arms and legs. The average height of adults with achondroplasia is four feet.

And from the age of ten months to four years, I needed oxygen twenty-four hours a day because my lungs were still developing.

Dwarfism doesn't just affect your bones and your height. It can also affect internal organs like your lungs and heart.

Eventually I outgrew needing oxygen, but my arms and legs pretty much stayed the same. And that made me different.

I'm almost four feet tall, but I won't grow much taller. Since my arms are short, I make adjustments. I pull down a clothing rack designed for me when I get dressed.

Around the house I use a stool to get what I need, or I just ask my mom or dad to help. I can do whatever I put my mind to, and yes, sometimes that means relying on other people.

But we all rely on other people occasionally to get what we need.

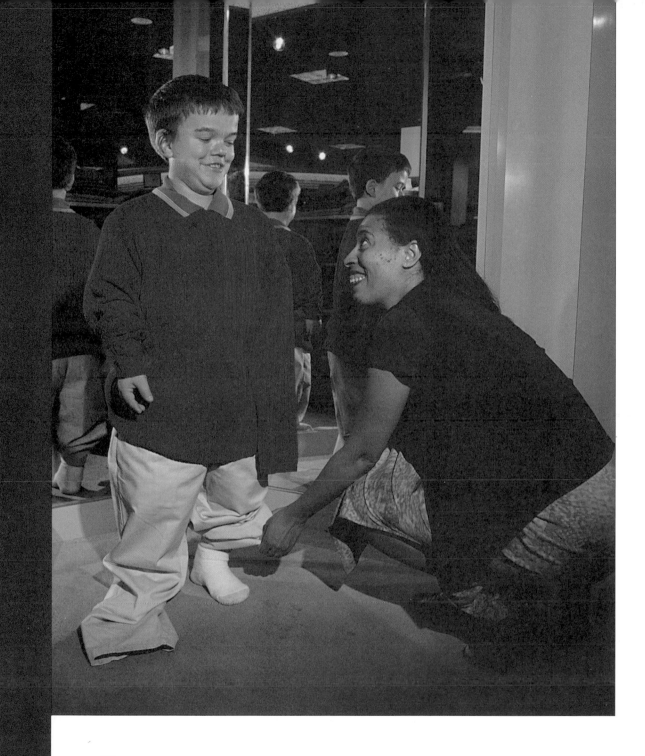

It's a little tricky buying clothes. I can wear the T-shirts and shorts I find in the store, but all my other clothes have to be altered in the arms and legs.

In fact, living in a tall world is a tall order. I have to ask for help in the grocery store if I need something on an upper shelf. I can't reach the counter at the deli, but I have no trouble buying tickets to the movies. Pay phones are okay, too.

Although I'm short,
I'm pretty strong.

I like sports. I bike, and
I'm learning how to play golf.
I love driving the cart—it's
just my size!

Home of the Mustangs

Okay— I know I'll never play pro basketball, but the game is my passion. I asked if I could be part of the school basketball team some way. They made me team manager. It's really exciting!

I can't wait to drive a car. I know I'll need a few special adjustments. I'll need to have the seat raised so I can see the road, and I'll have to add extensions for the gas and brake pedals.

I won't be driving on my own for a little while, though. I'm still in junior high, at Denver Academy, a pretty cool school. The question I'm asked most often is how old I am and how come I'm so short. I say I'm fourteen, and I'm a dwarf.

I explain that it's only my height that makes me different. My heart and my brain are as big as anyone's.

I think I've made up for being short-statured by developing the confidence to talk to people and make them feel comfortable around me. I have a lot of friends. I can get along with just about anyone, and that has made me a leader at school.

Sure, it's easy to feel sorry for yourself when your friends are growing tall and you know you never will. And it still hurts when people stare at me because I'm a little person. But God made me this way. I can't change it, and I'm going to make the best of it. I refuse to let my size sell me short!

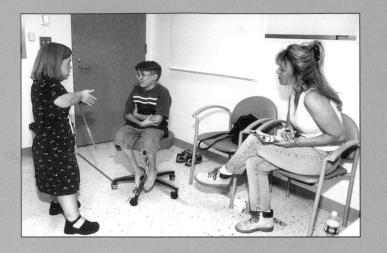

Ericka Peasley is a genetic counselor.

(Right) Bruce Johnson is an artist.

Whenen I'm older I want to be a commercial pilot. I know I can make my dream come true because I've seen so many success stories at the Little People of America national conferences. Once a year more than a thousand little people from around the world get together to meet friends, learn the latest medical information, and encourage each other to go for our dreams.

Kenneth Lee, M.D., is a doctor specializing in diseases of the digestive organs.

Mark Andrews is sports director and a radio announcer for a radio program heard throughout the country.

Laura Zirpolo is a manager with a health insurance company.

Mark Trombino, a technical recruiter, and Anu Singh, an engineer for a software company, are engaged to be married.

Dan Okenfuss is a political analyst.

The biggest lesson I've learned is that everyone faces challenges. Some are on the outside; some are on the inside, where no one can see.

Take my friend Tony. He has a reading disability. School is a real challenge, but that doesn't stop him from being an honor student.

My friend Leslie says, "My biggest challenge is that I'm really, really shy. Josh helps bring me out of my shell because he's so positive and has a great attitude. He's taught me just to be myself. The more comfortable you are with yourself, the more comfortable the world will be with you."

My friend Jim says, "I'm sure it's hard for Josh to walk as far as we do and always have to look up at everyone. But the truth is we look up to him for going for whatever he wants in life and not being afraid someone might laugh at him."

I've known Jim the longest of my friends, and we made a promise to each other when we first met . . .

that no matter where we go
or what we do, we will

never sell ourselves short!

About Dwarfism

Dwarfism is a medical condition that results in short stature. Because dwarfism limits physical growth, particularly in the arms and legs, a person with dwarfism may reach an adult height of only four feet, ten inches. Dwarfism most often is caused by a genetic mutation that occurs as the baby is beginning to form inside the mother. Even scientists do not know exactly why the mutation occurs. But evidence shows that people with dwarfism have been a part of the human condition as long as humans have inhabited the planet. People with dwarfism have even appeared in ancient Egyptian hieroglyphics and paintings from the Middle Ages.

The most common form of dwarfism, achondroplasia, occurs in one of every twenty thousand to forty thousand births, making it fairly rare. A boy like Josh might be the only person with dwarfism in his school or even his town. Fortunately, through an organization called LPA, Inc. (Little People of America), Josh and his parents can meet other families affected by dwarfism. LPA provides a forum for learning about dwarfism, coping with its social and emotional challenges, and finding expert medical care.

As we move into the twenty-first century, educational and employment opportunities for people with dwarfism abound. We hail from all walks of life and ethnic backgrounds. The dwarf population is diverse, much like society at large, and is comprised of physicians, lawyers, politicians, engineers, plumbers, actors, homemakers, ministers—just about any profession imaginable.

Born to a world made for people over five feet tall, Josh, like many people with dwarfism, has had to adapt his environment to get things done—whether it's standing on a stool to brush his teeth, adjusting his closet so he can reach his clothes, or, one day, using pedal extensions to drive a car.

Despite his height, Josh has shown us that people with dwarfism are pretty much like everyone else, with the same hopes and dreams of creating a life filled with excitement and meaning. As you can see by reading his story, short stature places no limits on the spirit and determination of those born with dwarfism.

Leroy Bankowski
President, LPA, Inc.

Stephanie Riggs is a TV journalist in Denver. She loves her job because she gets to meet cool people like Josh who remind us every day to stand tall, believe in ourselves, and accept each other's differences.

Bill Youmans has been a professional photographer for twenty-one years. He joined this project because he so admired the way Josh has met his challenges. Bill lives in Denver.

If you would like more information about little people, call LPA, a nonprofit organization that provides support and information to people of short stature and their families.

You can call LPA toll free at 888-LPA-2001 or e-mail them through their Web site at www.lpaonline.org. Their address is Box 745, Lubbock, TX 79408. Bill and Stephanie will give their profits from this book to this vital organization.